Developing Sustainable Neighborhoods
For Today's Housing Market

A Case Study Handbook

Mid Atlantic Cohousing

Zev Paiss & Neshama Paiss, Editors

First Edition Published Under a Grant
From Wallace Global Fund

Revised Edition

Sharon Villines
Editor & Designer

Developing Sustainable Neighborhoods
For Today's Housing Market
A Case Study Handbook
Revised Edition

Mid Atlantic Cohousing

Mid Atlantic Cohousing
info@midatlanticcohousing.org
http://www.midatlatniccohousing.org
866-620-2646

Mid Atlantic Cohousing is a non-profit, 501(c)3 corporation dedicated to informing and educating the public about cohousing, acting as a clearinghouse for information about cohousing and providing support for forming, building, and built cohousing and other intentional communities in the Mid Atlantic United States.

Graphic Design: Sharon Villines

Cataloging:

Mid Atlantic Cohousing: Developing Sustainable Neighborhoods for Today's Cohousing Market, A Case Study Handbook.

Revised Edition / Mid Atlantic Cohousing. Zev Paiss and Neshama Paiss, editors, first edition. Sharon Villines, editor, revised edition. Graphic Design: Sharon Villines.
p. cm.

Includes: Illustrations, bibliography.

ISBN

1. Cohousing. 2. Housing Cooperatives. 3. Neighborhood Development. 4. Residential Real Estate Development. 5. Leach, Jim. 6. McCamant, Katie. 7. Tucker, Don. 8. Eastern Village, Silver Spring MD. 9. Nevada City Cohousing, Nevada City CA. 10. Wild Sage Cohousing, Boulder CO. 11. Mid Atlantic Cohousing.

Acknowledgments

Mid Atlantic Cohousing thanks the following individuals, businesses, and organizations for their help in the production of the first edition of *Developing Sustainable Neighborhoods for Today's Housing Market*.

- To Jim Leach, Katie McCamant, and Don Tucker, the three developers who generously gave of their time to be filmed for the companion DVD and who were willing to share detailed information about their projects. *See the form at the back of the book to order the DVD.*
- To the members and residents of Eastern Village, Nevada City, and Wild Sage Cohousing for allowing us to film their neighborhoods and welcoming us into their homes. They demonstrated the openness that is a hallmark of cohousing.
- To Abraham Paiss & Associates, Inc., and to Zev & Neshama in particular, who wrote, filmed, directed, and produced the video, and researched, compiled, and wrote this Case Study Handbook.
- To the Cohousing Association of the United States for administrative support.
- To Wallace Global Fund whose financial support for the first edition made this possible.
- To Sharon Villines, editor and designer of the Revised Edition.
- And to the 250 other built and developing cohousing neighborhoods across the U.S. that demonstrate what this project is all about — helping create a sustainable future on our planet. With your help we know we can achieve this important goal.

We started this project to inform and inspire others to share our passion for living cooperatively in community while reducing our carbon footprint. It has been our honor to work on this project and, with the support of more builders and developers, may this lead to the development of hundreds of new cohousing communities in the years ahead.

We invite you to join us!

Martie Weatherly
Ann Zabaldo
Executive Producers

Table of Contents

Case Studies

Eastern Village Cohousing

Nevada City Cohousing

Wild Sage Cohousing

Cohousing Resources

Companion Video

And Last But Not Least

Mid Atlantic Cohousing

www.midatlanticcohousing.org
Info@MidAtlanticCohousing.org
866-620-2646

Introduction

On behalf of Mid Atlantic Cohousing, we are pleased to bring you the case study handbook, *Developing Sustainable Neighborhoods for Today's Housing Market.* We hope this handbook will provide the information you need to be assured that including cohousing in your building mix will be a profitable, low-risk investment and a contribution to green building and sustainable neighborhoods.

Inside, you will find three case studies, each presenting an award-winning green cohousing community:

- Eastern Village Cohousing, a 56-household mixed-income community in a converted office building in Silver Spring, Maryland. Developer: Don Tucker, Eco Housing Corporation.
- Nevada City Cohousing, a 34-household community in Nevada City, California. Developer: Kathryn McCamant, CoHousing Partners.
- Wild Sage Village, a 34-household mixed-income neighborhood in Boulder, Colorado. Developer: Jim Leach, Wonderland Hill Development Company.

Each case study includes detailed information about the developer and the project including the budget, architectural drawings, the energy-efficient features, and the advantages of the partnership between the developers and the future residents.

In addition, we have produced a DVD that includes

America may be more ready than ever to consider cohousing's benefits, which include about 25% to 50% less driving, 75% less land used fo``r housing, and at least 80% less energy used.

National Association of Home Builders (NAHB)

videos of all three communities and detailed interviews with the developers.

Green sustainable building is one of the few areas where there is strong economic growth in the housing industry. We also know that green building is no longer an option — it is imperative.

Cohousing communities are designed with green buildings and other green features. They also produce socially sustainable neighborhoods with strong, self-regulating homeowners associations. In addition, when cohousing projects have been included within larger master plan and New Urbanist towns, they offer clear advantages for the larger neighborhood where, as developer Jim Leach says, they are "the starter dough of community."

The companion DVD features the developers and projects presented in the handbook. They may be ordered from Mid Atlantic Cohousing in several ways.

Visit: http://www.MidAtlanticCohousing.org
Call: 866-620-2646
Email: DVD@MidAtlanticCohousing.org.

Please contact us for additional information or to schedule a phone call to learn more about cohousing neighborhoods.

Now more than ever, our country needs socially cohesive and environmentally sustainable communities. Are you the developer who will help build them?

Ann Zabaldo
Martie Weatherly
Executive Producers

What is Cohousing?

Cohousing is a residential neighborhood planned and managed by the residents. They may be new or rehabbed and urban, suburban, or rural. They range from small to large with the middle range being 30-40 homes. The homes may be single family detached, attached, stacked, or mult-family buildings.

Cohousing originated in Denmark in the early 1970's. This innovative neighborhood model was introduced to the United States in 1988. It is now one of the most promising solutions to many of today's challenging social and environmental concerns.

As cooperative inter-generational neighborhoods, cohousing communities balance the traditional advantages of home ownership with the benefits of shared facilities. The clustering of homes designed to protect privacy while encouraging interaction provides ongoing connections with neighbors.

A new cohousing model designed for active adults aged 50 and above is now developing in the United States called elder or senior cohousing. These communities are often located adjacent to inter-generational cohousing neighborhoods and provide a new model for living in the second half of life.

This view of Nevada City Cohousing is an example of how cohousing communities cluster homes along an internal pedestrian walkway and put parking on the periphery.

Six Primary Characteristics
That Cohousing Communities Share

Adapted from the Cohousing Association of the United States

1. PARTICIPATORY PROCESS

Future residents participate in the planning and
creation of the project so it meets their needs.
Increasingly, cohousing communities are initiating a
streamlined process based on a partnership between
a developer and the cohousing group. This makes the
project less risky and it can often be completed in a
shorter time. A well-designed, pedestrian-oriented
community without resident participation in the
planning process may be "cohousing–inspired," but it
is not a cohousing community.

2. NEIGHBORHOOD DESIGN

The site plan or physical layout and orientation of
the buildings encourages social interaction and
community. The homes are clustered on the site
leaving more shared open space. The homes typically
face each other along a pedestrian street or courtyard
and cars are parked on the periphery. The shared club
house or "common house" is often visible from the
front door of every dwelling. In cohousing, the design
of the neighborhood creates relationships between
the buildings and facilitates spontaneous connections
among neighbors.

3. COMMON FACILITIES

Common facilities, designed for daily use, are an
integral part of the community and supplement the
private residences. The common house typically
includes a large kitchen, dining area, sitting area,

children's playroom, laundry, library, exercise room, crafts room, guest rooms, and a workshop space. Most communities have playgrounds, common green areas, and community gardens. Since the buildings are clustered, larger suburban and rural sites may have several acres of shared open space. Urban communities may have green roofs, landscaped piazzas, and planted containers on balconies.

4. RESIDENT MANAGEMENT

Cohousing communities are managed by the residents, though a few hire help with some tasks. Members do most of the work required to maintain the property, participate in preparation of common meals, and meet regularly to develop policies that govern the community.

5. NON-HIERARCHICAL STRUCTURE AND DECISION-MAKING

In cohousing communities there are leadership roles, but no one person has authority over others. Most groups start with one or two "burning souls" and as people join the group, each person takes on responsibilities consistent with his or her skills, abilities, or interests. Most cohousing groups make all their decisions by consensus. Many groups also have a policy for voting if consensus cannot be reached, though it is rarely used.

6. NO SHARED COMMUNITY ECONOMY

The community is not a source of income for its members. Occasionally, a cohousing community will pay one of its members to do a specific (usually time limited) task, but more typically the task will simply be considered that member's contribution to the community.

What Makes Cohousing Sustainable?

Adapted from "Why is Cohousing Green" *by Wonderland Hill Development Company.*

Cohousing communities are models for sustainable living. These small-scale neighborhoods generally abide by the principle of "using less" and "sharing more." Values typical of cohousers include resource conservation, energy-efficiency, increased health of residents, and a cohesive social community. Additional sustainable elements include:

Community is the secret ingredient in sustainability.

Jim Leach
Wonderland Hill

Sites selected close to public transportation

Proximity to mass transit encourages residents to walk and bike more, reducing use of their personal automobiles. This cuts down air pollution and carbon emissions, while increasing personal health, and exercise. Research shows that cohousers drive up to 50% less after they move into cohousing. Sprawl is reduced by building where services already exist.

Site design optimizing land use by building a village with residents in close proximity

Higher density minimizes the built area and allows more people on a smaller footprint on the land. This provides opportunities for shared common areas, more social interaction among neighbors, and the preservation of open space.

Automobile parking located on the periphery

By separating parking from the pedestrian areas, cohousing communities are safer and less car dominated, thus encouraging more social interaction.

Homes and common house oriented to optimize solar opportunities

Cohousing neighborhoods use both active and passive solar methods increasing the use of renewable energy resources for daily activities.

Broad range of home sizes

Diversity is a prized quality of cohousing communities. Including a wide variety home sizes and prices ensures a more complex and inclusive social environment.

Landscaping mindful of ecology and water conservation

Cohousing residents create attractive landscaping while using native and water efficient plants in conjunction with irrigation zoning, cluster planting, sod reduction, and effective storm water management.

Home design to conserve energy and use ecologically sound materials, processes, and systems

Cohousing developers and community members consider both the carbon footprint and the indoor air quality of the home. Neighborhoods use a whole-systems approach to designing and building a home taking into account how and where materials were acquired and how they are installed. Cohousing homes are designed to be highly energy-efficient with adequate and durable insulation, sound deadening and insulated windows, and sufficient weather stipping and caulking. A well built, resource conserving home reduces energy bills and the overall life cycle costs of the home.

Shared centralized facilities and resources

A large multi-purpose common house has guest rooms,

children's play areas, workshops, exercise areas and other spaces which reduces the need for residents to have larger private homes. Neighbors frequently share lawn mowers, gardening and workshop tools, recreational equipment, washer and dryers, and large screen televisions in the common house. Households save money by not purchasing these individually.

Residents skillful at sharing resources and supporting one another.

Neighbors often establish cooperative arrangements for daily tasks such as childcare, cooking, running errands for one another, grounds maintenance, and repairs of the neighborhood. Shared activities save money for the residents and produce a strong and resilient community.

At Wild Sage Cohousing, homes are oriented to optimize active and passive solar energy use.

Eastern Village Cohousing

On the Reverse:

The courtyard at Eastern
Village Cohousing is a
landscaped pedestrian walk
and garden that covers the
ground source loops for
the geothermal heating
and cooling system. It was
formerly the parking lot for
the office building that was
renovated as 56 residential
and 11 live/work artist
spaces.

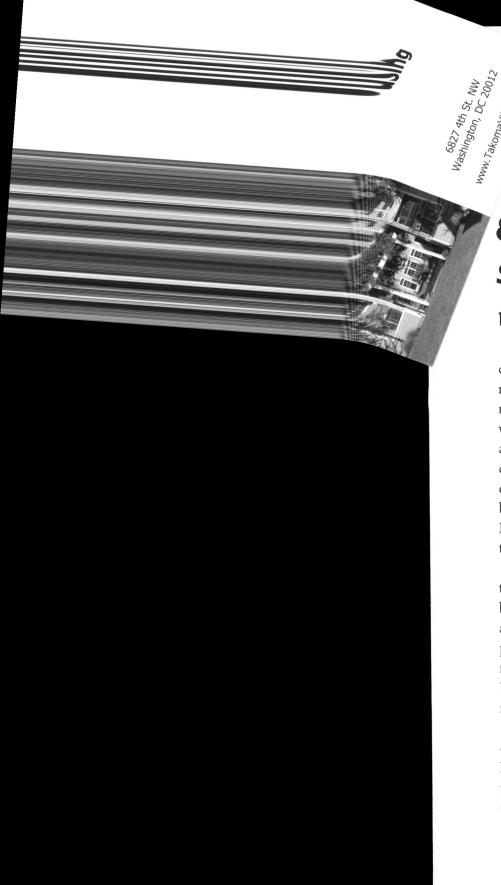

6827 4th St. NW
Washington, DC 20012
www.TakomaVillage.org

Eastern Village Cohousing

Silver Spring, Maryland

Project Overview

Eastern Village Cohousing is a planned urban community designed to feel like a village. The mixed residential and commercial project includes 56 residential units with an additional 11 units of live/ work artist spaces. The project is a gut rehab of an abandoned 40-year old four-story office building in downtown Silver Spring, Maryland, on the boundary of Washington D.C. Eastern Village is noteworthy for being the first Leadership in Energy and Environmental Design (LEED) Silver certified cohousing community in the United States.

The building is heated and cooled with a state-of-the-art geothermal system with ground-source loops buried under the courtyard. A green roof also serves as a recreation and sitting area for movies, wine and cheese parties, and spontaneous picnic dinners among the residents. The asphalt parking lot in the middle of the U-shaped office building has been transformed into a richly landscaped courtyard and community garden

There is no on-site parking. Residents use an adjacent county owned and operated parking lot. The residents have many more bikes than cars, however, frequently using the nearby bike paths or taking the Metro to work. Over 70% of the units were sold prior to construction.

Eastern Village residents have a management

It was great having a built in focus group of committed future residents. This allowed me to push the boundaries of sustainability because my buyers were involved from the very beginning.

Don Tucker
Eco Housing Corporation

company but retain many of the decisions themselves, using consensus and based on the following principles:

- We value ecological responsibility, sustainable design and a balance of aesthetics and affordability.
- We foster inter-connectedness, growth, care, communication, and respect among our membership.
- We engage responsibly with our neighborhood and the wider world.

About Silver Spring MD

Eastern Village is located in the new Downtown Silver Spring Arts and Entertainment Center, which is an SBA-designated HUBZone, a Historically Underutilized Business Zone.

It is within walking distance to:

- The Silver Spring Metro Station
- The MARC commuter train
- Many retail shops
- A wide variety of restaurants
- Several grocery stores
- Discovery Communications Headquarters
- NOAA, the National Oceanic and Atmospheric Administration
- Montgomery College
- The American Film Institute

Under development nearby is a showcase urban bicycle and pedestrian greenway, the Metropolitan Branch Trail of the National Park Service's Rivers & Trails project. The Branch Trail will link Silver Spring MD, to Union Station in downtown Washington DC.

Takoma Village Cohousing consists of 43 p... flats clustered around a central piazza and green. We ... and the richness of intergenerational living. ... a vibrant community life centered around exchanging together to maintain the buildings and grounds, ...residents enjoy ... socializing. We make decisions by consensus. ...port, working ... common house, which includes a large ...l meals, and ... TV and reading areas, exercise room, ... nur ... surrounding neighborhood offers ... Metro's Red Line.

Developer

Donald E. Tucker, LEED, AIA
President, Eco Housing Corporation

Don has over 30 years of experience developing housing, from small group homes for seniors to large multifamily complexes. He is a registered AIA architect and real estate developer, and a recognized expert in the programming, design, and development of multifamily, senior, and special-user housing. Don's knowledge of real estate development enables him to assist clients with site procurement, feasibility studies, financing, and development coordination.

Prior to 1974, Don was associated with several prominent architectural firms in Philadelphia and San Francisco. He received a Bachelor of Architecture degree from the University of New Mexico in 1968, and was awarded a Fellowship in Urban Design at the University of California, Berkeley, where he received a Master's Degree in Architecture in 1970. He taught architecture at Temple University, lectured at numerous conferences, and has written articles on affordable housing and senior housing design.

Don is cofounder and principal of affordable housing developers, AHD, Inc., and the environmental design group, EDG Architects, LLC. Eco Housing Corporation provides a full range of development services including project development, architecture, engineering, and project management. Using the cohousing model of consensus building, the firm works closely with the residents to develop a design program and budget.

ēcohousing

**Don Tucker,
President
Eco Housing**
2 Bethesda
Metro Center, #707
Bethesda, MD 20814
www.ecohousing.net
Info@ecohousing.net
(301) 654-6670

Awards for Eastern Village Cohousing

- **2007 Certificate of Recognition for Design Excellence in Affordable Green Housing.** AIA Housing & Custom Residential Knowledge Community, and the AIA Center for Communities of Design

- **2006 Livable Communities Green Roof of the Year.**

- **2005 Green Project of the Year Award.** National Association of Home Builders (NAHB), Green Builders for Luxury Multi-family Homes

- **2005 Excellence in Design Award for Multi-Use Residential Development.** Environmental Design + Construction Magazine.

- **First Place. Affordable Housing Conference**, Montgomery County, MD

- **LEED Silver** Rating for Environmental Performance by the U.S. Green Building Council

- **2003 Smart Growth Award.** Smart Growth Alliance

The paint splattered, unattractive, unused, black asphalt roof became . . .

. . . a luxurious gazebo, children's playground, garden, and green roof.

PROJECT DETAILS

ADDRESS: 7981 Eastern Avenue, Silver Spring, Maryland 20910

LOCATION: Urban

BUILDING TYPE: Adaptive reuse and renovation of 1957 office building

LOT SIZE: .70 acre site

FINISHED AREA: 92,600 square feet

NUMBER OF HOMES: 56 residential condominium units

HOME SIZES: 634 sq. ft. one bedroom flats to 1,580 three bedroom lofts

ECONOMICS: Mixed-income with 7 moderately priced homes; half of the initial sales were workforce housing between 80-100% of AMI

MASS TRANSIT: Neighborhood is .6 miles to Metro stop and across the street from a local bus stop

ORIGINAL SALES PRICE: $220-$320 per square foot

SIZE OF COMMON HOUSE: 6,000 square feet, 3 levels with elevator

COMPLETED: July 2005

DEVELOPER: Eco Housing Corporation, Bethesda, MD

ARCHITECT: EDG Architects, Bethesda, MD

BUILDER: Meridian Construction, Gaithersburg, MD

TOTAL PROJECT COST: $11,995,000

COMMUNITY WEBSITE: www.easternvillage.org

COMMUNITY DEMOGRAPHICS AT MOVE-IN: 85 adults, 15 children

ADDITIONAL: First cohousing building to be LEED certified by the U.S. Green Building Council

Green Features

Adaptive Reuse

Renovation of 40-year old unused office building with environmental quality a high priority.

Location

Urban rehab development in downtown Silver Spring where the Metro train line, shopping, restaurants and services are within a 10-minute walk. A large grocery store and shopping center are a short walk away.

Energy-Efficiency Ratings

LEED Silver Certification awarded in September 2005, making Eastern Village the first LEED-certified cohousing building.

Green Roof

Living green roof helps control rainwater runoff and reduces cooling loads. Additional cooling provided by front façade with a "green screen" sunshade. The roof has an R-23.6 value at the green roof and R-25 at the pavers.

A walkway through the living green roof at Eastern Village Cohousing

Mass Transit

Easy access to public transportation, .6 miles from the Metro station and across the street from a bus stop. A pedestrian rather than automobile emphasis with no parking on site, homes adaptable for home office use, and extensive storage areas for bicycles.

Geothermal Heating and Cooling

Each unit is served with high-efficiency ground-source heat pumps connected to a common circulation loop.

A series of 45 650-feet wells allow individual water source heat pumps to exchange heat with the earth.

Water Conservation

Low-flow faucets, shower heads, and toilets. Interior plumbing fixtures use 20% less water than conventional condominium buildings. Shower heads use less than 2.2 gallons per minute. Rain barrels collect rain water from the building's down sprouts.

Construction Waste

The general contractor managed a successful on-site construction waste recycling program with over 52% waste materials or 1,206.4 tons diverted from a landfill. All original fluorescent lamps were recycled.

Sustainable Materials

Use of recycled and rapidly renewable materials, including metal studs, carpet, roof membrane, metal stairs, drywall, and welded-wire trellis system. Regionally manufactured materials used when possible, conserving transportation resources.

Transformed Parking Lot

The courtyard, originally a paved parking area, transformed into a resident amenity with native plants and light-colored concrete to minimize the project's contribution to the urban heat-island effect.

Efficient Insulation

Wall insulation was added as part of the retrofit for an improved building envelope.

Appliances

Residents agreed to use only Energy Star refrigerators and freezers, initially and as replacement. Low water dishwashers and washing machines save 35% water usage compared to standard appliances.

Windows & Doors

Used high performance windows and doors with an energy efficiency rating of greater than R-21.

Lighting

Interior lighting consists of compact fluorescent fixtures with some standard incandescent fixtures. Exterior lighting is low-level

Finishes

Odor-free paints, low-emitting finishes.

Ecosystem Restoration

Site is replanted with Maryland native and adaptive plants in the courtyard and green roof, minimizing turf area and eliminating the need for a permanent irrigation system.

Flooring

Recycled carpets, linoleum and bamboo flooring.

Over 1,000 tons of removed construction materials were diverted from landfills during the building of Eastern Village.

Recycling

On-site recycling containers for residents.

Products

The residents have a commitment to use environmentally-friendly housekeeping products.

Designed for Community

Residents have two open spaces for socializing in the courtyard and on the roof, in addition to the Common House.

Each unit at Eastern Village has its own balcony that looks over the courtyard. Flower boxes line the tops of the balcony rails.

Project Budget

Project Cost:	$11,995,000
Admin & Legal	$54,000
Permits & Fees	$91,000
Design & Engineering	$304,500
Common Facilities	$1,130,000
Land Acquisition	$2,891,400
Marketing*	$325,000
Project Management Fees	$150,000
Financing Costs	$750,000
Cost Incurred at Closing	$244,000
Construction Costs	$5,431,042
Insurance	$45,000
Profit	$1,684,000
Total Sales	$13,679,000

The marketing budget includes education, training, sales, and community building for the future resident group.

Additional Financial Information:

Units sold prior to construction: 70%

Percentage of investors: 13.3% (Developer)

Bank financing: 86.7%

Project earned the LEED-Silver Certification which enabled it to gain Maryland Commercial Tax Credits

Montgomery County provided a $100,000 grant for Green Screen façade installation and upkeep

A living Green Screen provides natural shading during hot summer months.

Architectural Plans
Drawings by EDG Architects

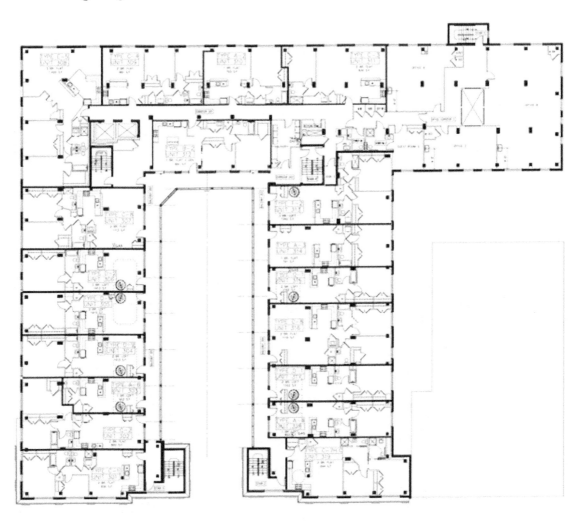

Third and Fourth Floor Unit Plans

Residential Floor Plans

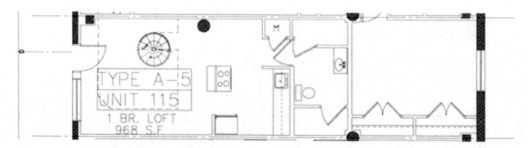

1 Bedroom Loft 968 sq ft.

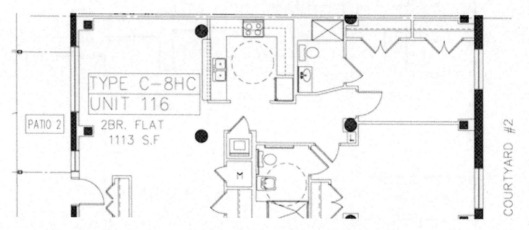

2 Bedroom Flat 968 sq ft.

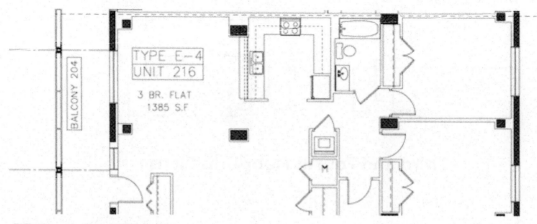

3 Bedroom Flat 1,385 sq ft.

Common Facilities

Eastern Village has a large area of adjacent common spaces on the first floor that include a living room, kids room, kitchen, and dining room. It also has common facilities throughout their building with rooms on each floor and areas in hallway nooks.

Common House

6,000 square feet on first Floor

Total Features include:

Wheel chair access
Large kitchen
Large dining area
Three guest rooms
Exercise/Yoga room
Toddler room
Teen room
Laundry area
Library
Multi-purpose room
Storage
Meditation room
Computer nook

Additional Common Areas:

Green Roof
Social and kid's play space
Covered gazebo
Courtyard
Native plants
Tool storage
Workshop

Nevada City Cohousing

On the Reverse

The central walkway around
which the 34 homes of Nevada
City Cohousing are clustered.

Nevada City Cohousing
Nevada City, California

Project Overview

Nevada City Cohousing is a multi-generational community of 34 households in California's Gold Rush town of Nevada City. This "brownfield" site, midway between Lake Tahoe and Sacramento, is where hydraulic mining was invented. Developer Katie McCamant liked the challenge of restoring the site whose soil was devastated by the washing away of hillsides in the 1860s and preserving six acres of woods as open space for community enjoyment.

Today, residents range from newborns to elders with lots of activity on the pedestrian path weaving throughout the neighborhood. The path begins at a main entrance with a two-level 4,000 square foot brightly-colored Common House and a large community outdoor deck overlooking a well-used swimming pool. From there you walk by richly landscaped lanes with clusters of red, blue and yellow and green town homes of Victorian and "Mother Lode" (mining inspired) architecture. On any given day you may see residents tending a large community vegetable garden, children collecting eggs from resident hens in the chicken coop, or teens and grandparents shooting pool in the Common House. The land was purchased in July 2002, construction began in 2004, and all 34 homes were pre-sold with a

"Over 90% of our market rate buyers moved out of single-family detached homes. They were looking for a more environmental and socially sustainable lifestyle."

Katie McCamant
CoHousing Partners

sizable waiting list prior to the start of construction.

In its community documents, Nevada City Cohousing states "active participation is a prerequisite for having a successful cohousing community." Adult residents work together on a collaborative basis to run the homeowners association. Adult members agree to attend regular community business meetings, be part of the common meals rotation, serve on at least one committee, and participate in the maintenance and improvement of the property.

About Nevada City

Nevada City is in the Sierra Nevada foothills, ringed by deep green hillsides and the Tahoe National Forest. It is minutes from the Sierra lakes and rivers, and trails for hiking and biking.

Nevada City was one of the California Gold Rush towns. The current population is 2,800 but in 1850, there were 10,000. The downtown area is an award-winning historic district listed in the National Register of Historic Places. With its historic 19th century architecture, it is considered to be among the best-preserved towns of the West.

Historic Nevada City Chamber of Commerce Home Page
http://www.nevadacitychamber.com/

Developer

Kathryn McCamant
President, CoHousing Partners

In the 1980s, Katie pioneered cohousing design and development in North America after she studied architecture in Denmark and published the book *Cohousing: A Contemporary Approach to Housing Ourselves,* which she co-authored with her husband Charles Durrett. She has been the lead project manager on six communities in California, overseeing these projects from site search through move in. Her work has been covered on ABC-TV, NBC-TV, CNN, The New York Times and many others.

Katie is a licensed architect who graduated with a Bachelor of Arts in Architecture from UC Berkeley. She did her graduate work, at the Royal Academy of Art and Architecture in Copenhagen. At McCamant & Durrett Architects she designed dozens of cohousing communities in the U.S. She now heads the CoHousing Partners team, overseeing the firm's projects, leading key training exercises, and serving as a liaison to the architecture and design consultants. CoHousing Partners is a full service residential development firm, specializing in cohousing communities. Their services include:

- Site Acquisition
- Participatory Design
- Community Building
- Financial Systems
- Project Management
- Master Planned Neighborhoods

**Kathryn McCamant,
President
Cohousing Partners**
241 Commercial Street
Nevada City, CA 95959
Info@CohousingPartners
www.CohousingPartners.com
(530) 478-1970

McCamant & Durrett Cohousing Awards

- **2009 Award of Merit.** American Institute of Architects (AIA) and American Association of Homes and Services for the Aging (AAHSA). For affordable senior housing for Silver Sage Cohousing in Boulder, CO. Completed for Wonderland Hill Development Co. with Bryan Bowen Architects.

- **2008 Best of 50+ Housing Award.** National Association of Homebuilders (NAHB) for Silver Sage Cohousing, Boulder, CO.

- **2008 Silver Energy Value Housing Award.** National Association of Homebuilders (NAHB), most energy-efficient multi-family housing project completed in 2007, for Nevada City Cohousing.

- **2006 Energy Value Housing Award.** National Association of Home Builders (NAHB), in conjunction with the U.S. Department of Energy, Multi-Family Category: Hot Climate, for Frogsong, Cotati Cohousing, Cotati, CA.

- **2005 Best New Housing Award of Excellence.** Berkeley Design Advocates for Sacramento Senior Homes, Berkeley, CA.

- **2004 Best in American Living Award.** Best Smart Growth Community. National Association of Home Builders, for FrogSong, Cotati Cohousing, Cotati, CA.

- **2004 Design Award Citation.** American Institute of Architects, Redwood Empire Chapter, for Cotati Cohousing, Cotati, CA.

- **2003 Best of Sonoma County.** Land Use & Transportation Coalition for Cotati Cohousing, Cotati, CA.

- **2001 Mixed-Use/Mixed Income Development Award.** American Institute of Architects for East Lake Commons Cohousing, Atlanta, GA.

Gravel parking lot at Nevada City Cohousing minimizes the use of asphalt

Green Features

Location

Site located near mass transit with local bus stop adjacent to property. Walking distance from downtown Nevada City wth restaurants, services, doctor offices and businesses available without getting into a car.

Photovoltaic System

PV panels on all the homes and the Common House. PV system will meet 80% of the community's electric needs and many resident have negative electric bills.

Passive Solar Heating

Optimum solar gain is achieved through the solar orientation of the buildings; recycled cellulose super insulation; perimeter foundation insulation; energy-efficient windows; and radiant barriers throughout

Photovoltaic cells on the roof at Nevada City Cohousing.

Active Solar Heating

Homes were pre-plumbed for solar panels to feed into a single boiler serving 3-6 homes for hydronic heating and domestic hot water. Energy bills are $20-$30 per month as compared to about $150 per month for an average energy bill in the area.

Low Toxicity Materials

Bamboo flooring; cellulose insulation; low toxic paint; low VOC adhesives and sealants; low formaldehyde materials; Tectum recyclable acoustic tiles in the Common House.

Water Conservation

Low water use fixtures in each home; dual flush toilets (savings of 4,000 gallons per toilet per year alone).

Responsible Forestry

Sustainably harvested framing lumber with almost no clear cut lumber (FSC certified); advanced framing using 25% to 40% less lumber to build the same square footage and less than half the lumber in a typical new house.

Minimal Asphalt

Autos are limited to the entrance of the community which minimizes the need for asphalt while the gravel parking area slows water run off.

Sustainable Waste Stream Management

No vinyl flooring; refinishable Marmoleum floors made of cellulose and linseed oil which composts into land fills. Low construction waste; recycled cellulose.

Minimum Impact

Minimum grading and tree removal; 60% of the site has been preserved as open space.

Responsible Landscaping

More than 90 new trees planted; indigenous grasses and wildflowers used throughout neighborhood; minimum water use and other key permaculture principles applied; on-site drain water management with bio-swale; water retention on-site.

Energy-Efficient Appliances

Energy Star fixtures and compact florescent bulbs

Project Details

Address: 200 Red Bud Way, Nevada City, CA 95959

Location: Small town setting

Building Type: New Construction

Lot Size: 11-acre site with six acres kept as open space, and seven single family lots sold separately

Number of Homes: 34 residential attached condominium units

Home Sizes: 858 sq. ft. one-bdrm flats to 1,694 four-bdrm townhouses

Economics: Mixed-income neighborhood with 29 market rate and five affordable homes

Original Home Prices: $255,000 to $450,000

Mass Transit: Neighborhood next to a local bus stop

Original Sales Price: $268 per square foot

Size of Common House: 4,160 square feet including workshop space

Parking: 16 garages plus 4 carports

Completed: May 2006

Development Team: A partnership between McCamant & Durrett Architects; the resident group, Nevada City Cohousing Group, LLC; and Wonderland Hill Development Company
Architect: McCamant & Durrett, Nevada City and Berkeley, CA

Builder: Tintle, Inc., Nevada City, CA

Community Website: www.nccoho.org

Community Demographics: 56 adults, 36 children

Additional: Location of first hydraulic gold mining in 1860's.

Project Budget

Project Cost:	$11,880,000
Admin & Legal	$237,000
Permits & Fees	$560,000
Design & Engineering	$623,400
Common House Furnishings	$100,000
Land Acquisition	$622,000
Marketing	$213,500
Project Management Fees	$729,500
Financing Costs	$460,000
Cost Incurred at Closing*	$283,000
Construction Costs	$7,150,000
Developer Warrenty	$50,000
Insurance	$513,600
Contingency	$328,000
Total Sales	$13,588,000
Developer Fee	$854,000
ROI to Community**	$854,000

*Discounts to buyers for early investment
** Community raised all equity investment

Additional Financial Information:

Homes pre-sold prior to construction 100%
Percentage member equity in project   15%
Percentage of outside investors   .09%
Bank financing 72% of value; 80% of costs

The site purchase and equity requirements were financed entirely by the residents themselves.

The 11-acre site includes six acres of preserved wooded open space

The 11-acre site at Nevada City allows the community to keep chickens and to have a swimming pool.

Architectural Plans
by McCamant & Durrett Architects

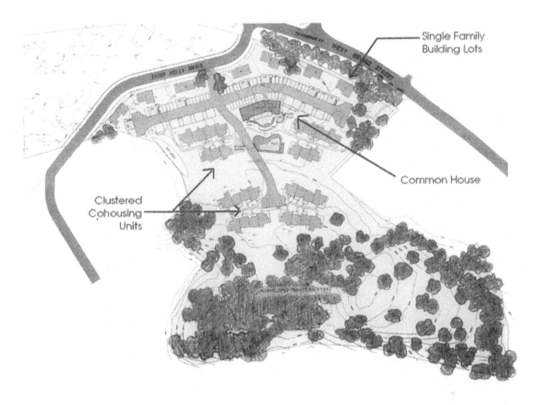

The 11-acre site at Nevada City Cohousing includes six acres of preserved wooded open space.

Common Facilities

Common House Details

Total of 4,160 sq. ft.
3,920 sq. ft. two-level building
240 sq. ft. workshop area

Common House Features

Wheelchair access
Photovoltaic panels
Large kitchen
Large dining area
Two guest rooms
Exercise/Yoga room
Toddler room
Teen room
TV/Media area
Laundry facilities
Library
Pool table
Storage

Additional Common Areas

Common plaza and green
Pool with solar hot water
Children's outdoor play space
Six acres of forest
Community garden
Hot tub
Tool shed
Chicken coop

**Common House
Second Floor Plan
960 sq. ft.**

Common House

First Floor Plan
2960 SQ FT

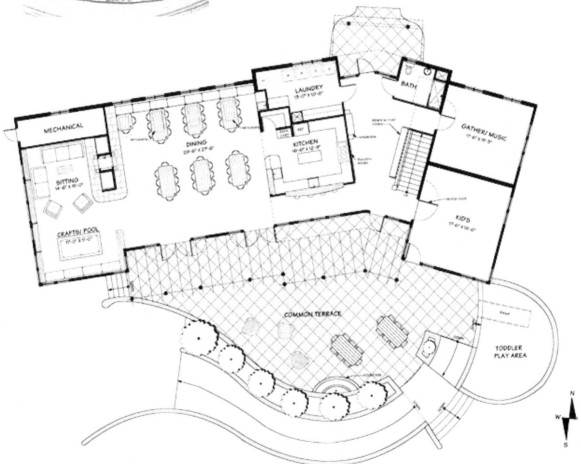

Residential Floor Plans
Two Bedroom Units

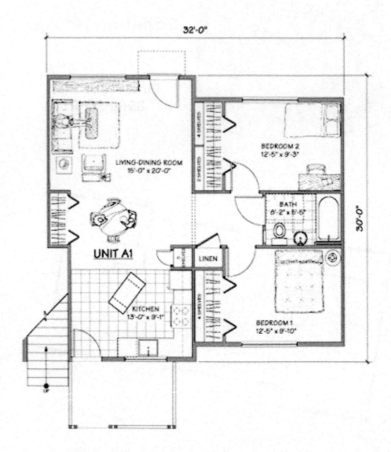

Upstairs, Two Bedroom Flat 858 sq ft.

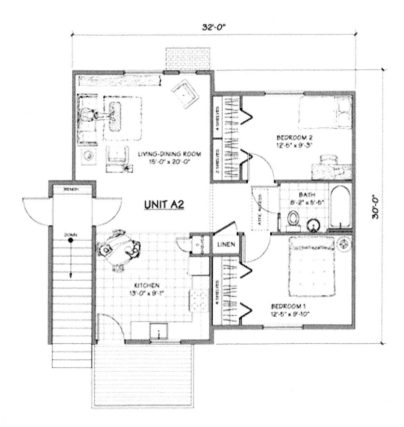

32'-0"

30'-0"

LIVING-DINING ROOM
15'-0" x 20'-0"

BEDROOM 2
12'-6" x 9'-3"

UNIT A2

BATH
8'-2" x 5'-5"

BENCH

DOWN

LINEN

KITCHEN
13'-0" x 9'-1"

BEDROOM 1
12'-6" x 9'-10"

Downstairs, Two Bedroom Flat 870 sq ft.

Four Bedroom Townhouse, 1694 sq. ft.

Townhouse, Upper Floor

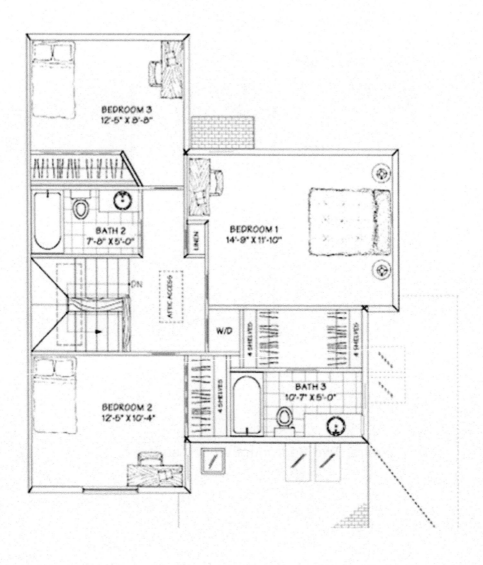

Townhouse, Lower Floor

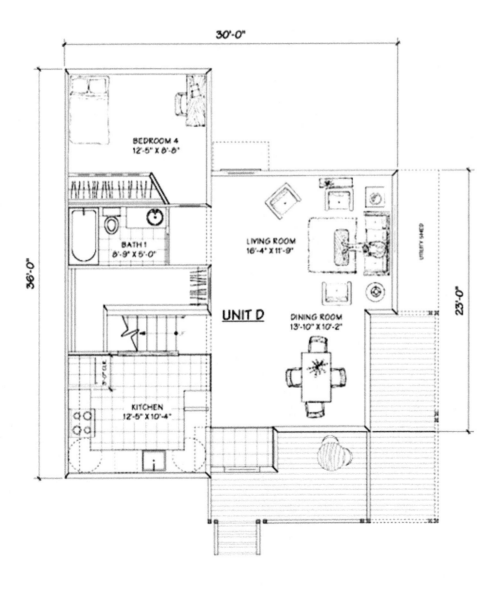

30'-0"

36'-0"

23'-0"

BEDROOM 4
12'-5" X 8'-8"

BATH 1
8'-9" X 5'-0"

UNIT D

LIVING ROOM
16'-4" X 11'-9"

UTILITY SHED

DINING ROOM
13'-10" X 10'-2"

KITCHEN
12'-5" X 10'-4"

Wild Sage Cohousing

On Reverse:

The 34 homes in Wild Sage Cohousing are arranged around a green and carefully oriented to maximize solar gain and minimize winter shading.

Wild Sage Cohousing
Boulder, Colorado

Project Overview

Wild Sage was a joint venture of 34 households committed to reclaiming the comfort and safety of a tight-knit community while living lightly on the land. The architect and the developer used a consensus process in which community members participated in the site planning and architectural design of their homes. The partnership between the future resident group and the professional development team produced solid agreements about density and open space, and community and privacy that allowed the project to meet the sustainability expectations of the group members while also enhancing their quality of life.

The site design concentrates building density on the perimeter, preserving the interior of the 1.5-acre site in a layered system of private patios, semiprivate garden corridors, and a community green. The common house, a contemporary club house, has one face to the shared courtyard and the other to the street. In addition to regular business meetings and social activities, optional community meals are held in the common house twice a week. The community also uses the common house to host neighborhood events, including meetings of the Holiday Neighborhood homeowners' association, the New Urbanist development of which they are a part. It is also available for private events. From the beginning,

"Cohousing has allowed me to pursue my passion for creating sustainable communities. Residents drive an estimated 30% less, pay 50% less in utility bills, and use 40% less water than the average American."

Jim Leach, Wonderland Hill Development Company

the Wild Sage community made a commitment to be an integrated part of the larger New Urbanist village.

Like other cohousing communities, Wild Sage has a wide variety of unit sizes. The first four Habitat for Humanity homes built in a cohousing community are among the 40% permanently affordable options. The residents are diverse in income, age, family size, and cultural background, and include singles, families, couples, empty-nesters, and seniors.

Environmental values are an important part of the community's vision statement that includes a commitment to "... using sustainable materials and practices whenever possible, ... we look beyond ourselves, and our time, striving to create a better world for the seventh generation and beyond."

Wonderland Hill Development Company Awards

- **2005 Community Conservation Award**, Center for Resource Conservation
- **2005 Energy Value Housing Award**, Silver, NAHB and NREL for Frogsong Cohousing
- **2004 Energy Value Housing Award**, Silver, NAHB, Affordable category, for Wild Sage Cohousing
- **2004 Best in American Living Award**, Best Smart Growth Community, NAHB for Frogsong Cohousing
- **New Millenium Energy-Star Awards:** 2004 for Wild Sage Cohousing, 2003 for Casa Verde Commons, 2002 Hearthstone Cohousing

Developer

James Leach
President
Wonderland Hill Development Company

Jim Leach has more than 40 years of experience in the design, construction, and development of sustainable housing, cohousing, planned neighborhoods, and urban infill. He has been a spokesperson for the Solar Energy movement since the early 1980's. In 1997, he was inducted into the Built Green Hall of Fame by the Home Builders Association of Metropolitan Denver. His award-winning neighborhoods have been recognized by the US Department of Housing and Urban Development (HUD), the National Association of Home Builders (NAHB), the National Council of the Housing Industry, the Urban Land Institute, the Congress for the New Urbanism, and the Solar Energy Research Institute. He serves on the board of the Affordable Housing Alliance.

Jim holds a Bachelor of Architectural Engineering and Bachelor of Business Management from University of Colorado at Boulder, and a Master of Construction Engineering from Stanford University. He is a licensed Professional Engineer in Colorado and New Mexico.

He is the developer and a founding resident of the Silver Sage Village designed for active adults, located across the street from inter-generational Wild Sage. These two adjacent cohousing communities are the first American example of a model popular in Denmark where cohousing originated.

In 2009, Wonderland Hill was the largest developer of cohousing in the United States with 16 completed communities.

Wonderland
WONDERLAND HILL DEVELOPMENT CO

Jim Leach, President
Wonderland Hill
Development Company
4676 Broadway Blvd.
Boulder, CO 80304
Info@whdc.com
www.whdc.com
(303) 449-3232

Project Details

Address: 1650 Zamia Ave., Boulder, CO 80304

Location: Urban setting

Building Type: New Construction

Lot Size: 1.48-acre site

Number of Homes: 34 attached condominium units

Home Sizes: Seven sizes from 640 SF one bedroom flats to 2,700 SF three-bedroom town homes

Economics: Mixed-income project with 22 market rate homes, 8 permanently affordable & 4 volunteer-built Habitat for Humanity homes

Original Sales Prices: $125,000 to $480,000; $150-$200 per sq. ft.

Mass Transit: Within walking distance of city bus line

Size of Common House: 5,700 square feet, including workshop space

Parking: 48 parking spaces, 21 garages and 4 carports

Completed: February 2004

Developer: Wonderland Hill Development Co., Boulder, CO

Architect: Jim Logan Architects, Boulder, CO

Resident Architect: Bryan Bowen Architects, Boulder, CO

Builder: Drahota Construction Company, Fort Collins, CO

Community Website: www.wildsagecohousing.org

Community Demographics: 59 adults, 18 children

Additional: Located within the 25-accree New Urbanist Holiday Neighborhood.

Wild Sage is located in the Holiday Neighborhood named after the Holiday Drive-In Theater, which closed in 1988. The theater's sign, designed in 1953, has been preserved as an example of the 1950's "googie" style.

Green Features

Photovoltaic Panels on the roof were purchased with savings in energy costs. With the kilowatts produced by the panels and efficient use of electricity, the community has net zero electricity consumption.

Location

The project site is located in the 25-acre Holiday Neighborhood, an award-winning New Urbanist village in North Boulder known for sustainable design and built green technologies. Residents in the New Urbanist neighborhood are less dependent on their automobiles and find walking, biking, and taking mass transit to be convenient alternatives for travelling to shopping, restaurants, and services. Wild Sage is close to miles of open space hiking trails and Wonderland Lake Park with dramatic views of the Foothills of the Rocky Mountains.

Mass Transit

The community is a five-minute walk from a main city bus line that takes residents to downtown Boulder, a 10-minute ride away.

Photovoltaic System

The community used a portion of their profit share to install PV panels on the homes. Additional PV panels are being purchased through money saved on HOA energy bills. According to an energy study by green architect Jim Logan, the units at Wild Sage have 2 kW of PV and efficient electricity use to approach net zero energy consumption.

Passive Solar Design

The homes and the common house were designed for optimal solar access with a south facing orientation. Homes have solar rough-in capability and two buildings have installed thermal panels for solar hot water.

Hydronic Heating System

Energy-efficient hot water boilers reduce heat loss and minimize mechanical redundancy. Solar hot water collectors warm a shared tank, with natural gas backup for domestic hot water and heating of the homes. There is one boiler for up to seven units per building.

Energy-Efficient Windows

South windows are low-e, double-paned to reflect heat in the summer and keep heat inside in the winter.

Insulation

Wet blown R-21 insulation was used for walls, dry blown R-38 for ceilings, and R-50 for attic. R-13 was used for the foundation, perimeter foundation insulation, and radiant barriers throughout.

Design

Airtight construction of the homes was confirmed by blower door tests. Other energy saving features are the compact footprints and shared side walls that save energy and reduce heat and cooling costs.

Low Toxic Materials

Low VOC paints and adhesives and nontoxic finishes were used throughout.

Energy Efficient Lighting

Energy Star fixtures were used in all the homes and the common house; florescent bulbs, on the exterior and interior.

Water Conservation

Low water use fixtures were used and dual flush toilets were an option. Rainwater is channeled to irrigate the gardens, and runoff is returned to the earth in vegetated swales.

Sustainable Landscaping

Native and low water plants were used in the landscaping.

Ventilation

Residents were offered the option of an advanced ventilation system for improved air quality.

The dining room in the Wild Sage Common House.

Financial Information

Project Budget

Administration & Legal	$40,805
Permits & Fees	$617,059
Design & Engineering	$403,999
Common House Furnishings	$21,500
Land Acquisition	$1,008,000
Marketing*	$101,675
Project Management Fees	$412,745
Financing Costs	$254,307
Cost Incurred at Closing	$186,097
Construction Costs (Includes options)	$4,615,107
Warranty	$25,000
Profit	$381,561
Total Project Budget	**$8,647,807**

*The marketing budget includes education, training, sales, and community building for the future resident group.

Additional Financial Information

Profit Allocation

Percentage to Developer	50%
Percentage to Community	25%
Percentage to Investors	25%

Financing

Homes sold prior to construction:	70%
Percentage of member equity in project:	5%
Percentage of outside investors:	5%
Bank financing of total project costs:	75%

Architectural Drawings
By Jim Logan Architects

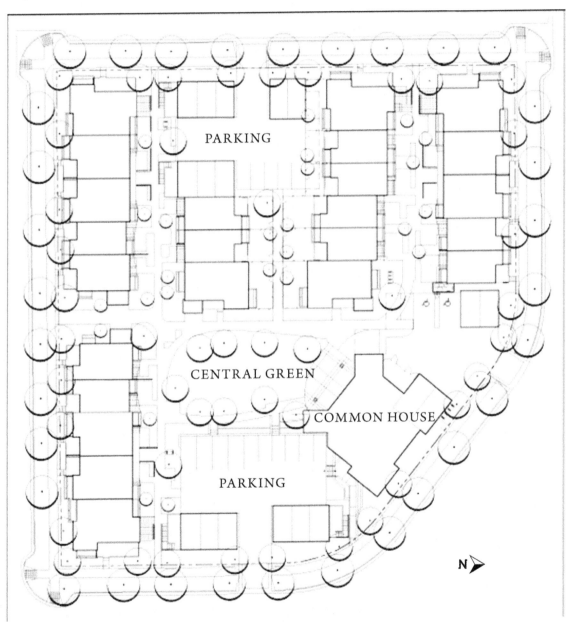

The 34 homes at Wild Sage Cohousing are clustered in five buildings. One parking area is on the periphery and the second next to the common house, which overlooks the green.

Common House

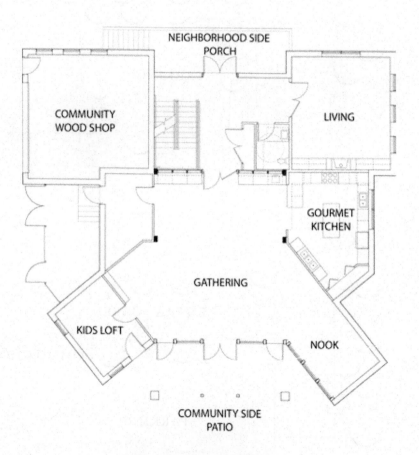

Upper Level / First Floor

Common House Features:

- 5700 Sq. ft.
- Wheelchair access
- Photovoltaic panels on roof
- Large kitchen
- Large dining area
- Two guest rooms
- Exercise & yoga room
- Toddler room
- Home theatre & media area
- Laundry facilities
- Library
- Storage
- Office

Additional Common Areas

- Workshop, fully equipped
- Tool shed
- Hot tub on roof deck
- Outside children's play area
- Common plaza and shared common green
- Recycling area
- Share one high speed internet connection

Lower Level / Basement

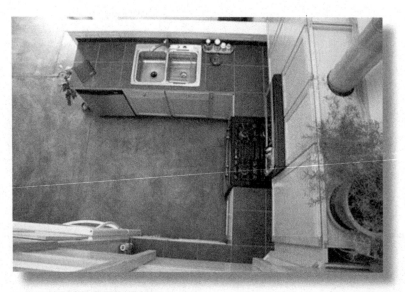

A Wild Sage residential kitchen
from a clerestory window.

Residential Floor Plans

3 Bedroom Town House
1,800 SF plus 900 SF Unfinished Basement

First Floor

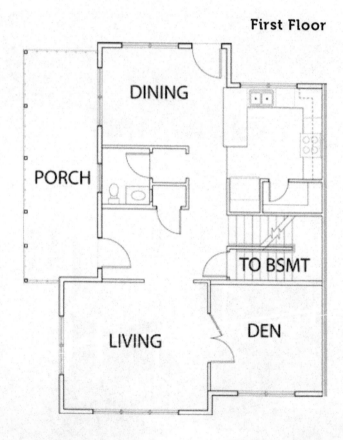

Second Floor

BED

BED

LAUNDRY

MASTER
BEDROOM

1 Bedroom
Carriage House
640 Square feet

BEDROOM

DINING + LIVING

PORCH

Cohousing Resources

On the reverse:

A hallway nook at Eastern
Village Cohousing is used as a
library.

Organizations

The Cohousing Association of the United States
Promotes the appreciation, understanding, and development of cohousing in North America. Free weekly e-newsletter. Many resources including contact information for developing and completed cohousing communities. Sponsors the annual National Cohousing Conference. http://www.cohousing.org.

Mid Atlantic Cohousing
Educates and informs the public about cohousing. Promotes, educates, and supports the efforts of people to create cohousing communities in the mid-Atlantic United States: District of Columbia, Maryland, North Carolina, Pennsylvania, and Virginia.

http://www.midatlanticcohousing.org.

Videos

Developing Sustainable Neighborhoods for Today's Housing Market

A 30-minute video for real estate development professionals. Executive producers: Mid Atlantic Cohousing. Funding provided by Wallace Global Fund. Written and produced by Abraham Paiss & Associates of Boulder, Colorado.

To order the DVD and Case Study Handbook visit:

http://www.MidAtlanticCohousing.org,

Email: DVD@midatlanticcohousing.org

Call (866) 620-2646.

Neighborhoods for People

An 18-minute introduction to the cohousing concept with interviews by residents and footage from cohousing communities across the United States. Abraham Paiss & Associates, Inc. 1995. To order visit:

http://www.AbrahamPaiss.com

Telephone: (303) 413-8066.

YouTube

There are also many videos on YouTube. Search on "Cohousing."

http://www.youtube.com

Books

Cohousing: A Contemporary Approach to Housing Ourselves
by Kathryn McCamant and Charles Durrett. Revised edition. (Berkeley: Ten Speed Press, 1994.)

"Cohousing and Shared Housing"
by Laura Bauer Granberry in *The World of Senior Living* edited by Pauline S. Abbott. (Baltimore: Health Professions, 2009).

The Cohousing Handbook: Building a Place for Community
by Chris ScottHanson and Kelly ScottHanson Revised edition. (Gabriola Island, BC: New Society Publishers, 2005).

Collaborative Communities: Cohousing, Central Living, and Other New Forms of Housing With Shared Facilities
by Dorit Fromm (NY: Van Nostrand Reinhold, 1991).

Creating A Life Together: Practical Tools to Grow Ecovillages and Intentional Communities
by Diana Leafe Christian (Gabriola Island, BC: New Society Publishers, 2003).

Developing Sustainable Neighborhoods for Today's Cohousing Market: A Case Study Handbook by Mid Atlantic Cohousing. Edited by Zev Paiss and Neshama Paiss. Revised edition edited by Sharon Villines. (Vienna, VA: Mid Atlantic Cohousing, 2010.)

Finding Community: How to Join an Ecovillage or Intentional Community
by Diana Leafe Christian (Gabriola Island, BC: New Society Publishers, 2007).

House by Tracy Kidder (Boston: Mariner Books, 1999).

Reinventing Community: Stories from the Walkways of Cohousing by David Wann (Golden, CO:Fulcrum, 2005).

The Senior Cohousing Handbook: A Community Approach to Independent Living by Charles Durrett. Second edition. (NY: New Society Publishers, 2009)

Toward Sustainable Communities: Resources for Citizens and their Governments by Mark Roseland, forward by Hazel Henderson (Gabriola Island, BC: New Society Publishers, 1998).

E-Mail Discussion Lists

Cohousing-L
About 500 members considering, developing, and living in cohousing discuss cohousing issues and offer advice. Excellent source of up-to-the-minute information about cohousing. Sign up at http://www.cohousing.org.

Elder Cohousing
  The discussion list of the Elder Cohousing Network. http://groups.yahoo.com/group/ElderCohousing/join.

Developing Sustainable Neighborhoods

Video

Written and Produced by Abraham Paiss & Associates
Boulder, Colorado

There is a video companion to *Developing Sustainable Neighborhoods* that includes interviews with all the developers featured in the *Case Study Handbook*, interviews with other cohousing professionals, and additional information on cohousing.

For more information on the DVD please contact Mid Atlantic Cohousing at:

www.midatlanticcohousing.org

Info@MidAtlanticCohousing.org

866-620-2646

And Last but Not Least

The Top 12 Reasons
to Develop Cohousing Communities

By Ann Zabaldo
Principal, Cohousing Collaborative, LLC
Ann@cohousingcollaborative.com

1. Straight developer-driven model: 70% or greater sell through prior to construction.

2. Joint Venture model: 70% or greater sell through prior to construction plus future residents contribute up to 15% of the cost of their unit to the project budget prior to construction.

3. Eliminates guess work — with a group in place you know in advance how many units and the types of units to build saving money and time.

4. The groups handles the marketing and outreach thereby significantly reducing this budget line item.

5. Eliminates issues around including low-income or affordable housing in the project. Cohousers welcome and seek out diversity in income. Cohousers will ASK to include a range of income levels in the project.

6. Reduce site acquisition costs. Because of the cohesive nature of cohousing you can build in "edge" areas. Cohousing is often on the "leading edge" in developing or redeveloping an area. It can serve as an anchor for future development.

7. Because cohousing uses clustering you can build on small parcels including very tight urban in-fill spaces.

8. Built-in focus group. You can easily test out design options saving money.

9. When addressing zoning boards or public meetings the residents go with you supporting your efforts and putting

a "face" project. They make the project real to the neighbors who are attending the meeting. You are not standing alone in a room of 150 or more irate people.

10.   Cohousers are early adopters. You can afford to be more creative, pushing the envelope on design and sustainability features because you already have committed buyers.

11.   Parking, which is so often an issue, is less so in cohousing because as a demographic, cohousers car share, use mass transit, bike or walk more than other homeowners. Reduces costs, surface run off/storm water management issues, design issues. (Parking space requirements will, of course, depend on your local zoning ordinances.)

12.   If done properly, inclusion of the residents in the development process combined with the consensus nature of cohousing, results in residents who are more likely to work out post-occupancy difficulties rather than hire lawyers.

CPSIA information can be obtained at www.ICGtesting.com
Printed in the USA
BVOW04s0500100916

461147BV00002B/2/P